Do It
(or Don't)

A
Boundary-Creating
Journal

by Kara Cutruzzula
illustrated by
Jasmina Zornić

ABRAMS IMAGE, NEW YORK

Introduction

Do you know what you want to do? Or do you let others *tell* you what you want to do?

Every day, we are faced with obligations, requests, and small demands. Some are easy to handle or appear like opportunities. Others might feel like burdens. Work items that carry too much weight. Creative ideas that never seem to move forward. And then, of course, there are those people who drain your energy.

And yet, we often keep churning along the same path, afraid to rock the boat, afraid to appear unkind, afraid to disappoint someone.

But what if the result is disappointing yourself?

I came to the realization lately that my inability to draw boundaries often led me to sacrifice my own creativity, skills, and future plans. Sometimes if you give up too much space to other people, you're left without any ground to stand on yourself.

Not anymore. In this journal, we're going to get incredibly clear on boundaries: How to create them, stick to them, and flourish within them. You might be feeling the urge to redraw some of your own boundaries, whether in your personal, professional, or creative life. Listen to this impulse. It's a sign you seek borders. And that's a very good thing.

THIS IS CLARITY. THESE ARE YOUR BOUNDARIES.

Because boundaries aren't restrictive—they can free you, and your future. Through establishing clear lines, you become aware of all you have to offer. No more over-extending yourself, overpromising, or stressing out because, once again, you said "yes" when you really should have said "no."

Boundaries keep you from burning out or giving too much. They help you give just enough—and leave plenty for yourself to keep going.

When's the last time you checked in with yourself?

Are you pulled in too many directions? Are you at a cross-roads? Are you overwhelmed by options and commit-ments? This is the moment to find clarity and connection again with your confident self. The one whose voice has been a little quiet. That person who isn't afraid to speak up and move forward with purpose and resolve.

It's time to let go of second-guessing and overanalysis. It's time to set some boundaries.

***

On a Tuesday morning, your phone pings. A good friend texts, "miss you, free tonight??" Going out sounds fun, except she's flaked on you three times in recent weeks . . . after you pushed aside other plans. And you suspect this might turn into another monologue about the job she hates. You want to be there for her, but you're also worried about returning home emotionally drained. What do you do?

It's a beautiful Friday afternoon and your boss messages you with a question: Can you create a new PowerPoint by Monday at noon? I mean, hypothetically, you *could*, but at what cost? You already have a pile of assignments to finish, and you can't bear to work through yet another weekend. What do you do?

It's Sunday morning and a collaborator calls to say they have a brilliant idea and asks if you want to churn out a new draft of that exciting project you've been working on together. And they would really love if you could do it right now. You want to be a team player, but you already have a full day. Plus, this isn't urgent. What do you do?

***

Our lives are full of these moments and situations requiring balletic navigation of our relationships, career arcs, and reputations. It's easy to want to be everything to everyone. It's much harder to put ourselves first. Is it even possible to find the perfect balance?

The answer is simple, but not easy: You either do it . . . or you don't. There is no in-between.

The art of creating boundaries is found in being decisive. It's *yes* or *no*, not *maybe*.

Knowing which answer to choose takes practice, trial and error, breaking old patterns, and prioritizing your own desires instead of defaulting to people-pleasing tendencies. Fantastic in theory, challenging in execution. Some patterns are so deeply ingrained that we barely realize

we're living them. But becoming aware of our actions and reactions is the first step. You begin to ask yourself, "Where is *my* line?" and "What do *I* need?"

In these pages, you'll work on creating clear boundaries around your time, habits, and projects. Revisit chapters when you feel they may be useful. Sit with the questions for as long as you need. And above all, stay honest. No one needs to see your responses but you.

Together, let's learn how to say *no* more often, flake gracefully, make room for what we need, and focus on our most vibrant and exciting futures. Creating boundaries *does* require work—but it's work that guides you toward freedom, happiness, and creativity. And it's work that happens not all at once, but in chapters.

Starting now, you'll define what you want to do. Decline what you *don't* want to do. Create the proper space to flourish. Learn to adapt but not go back. Lean in to ease. Ask for help. And, along the way, you will learn how to rest.

Do it—or don't. The choice is yours.

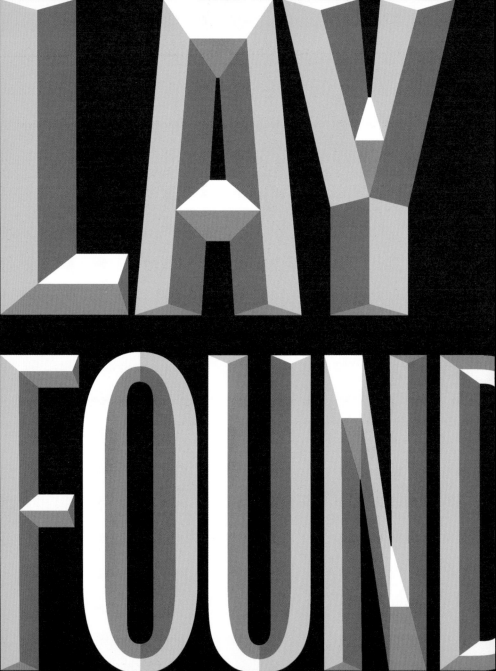

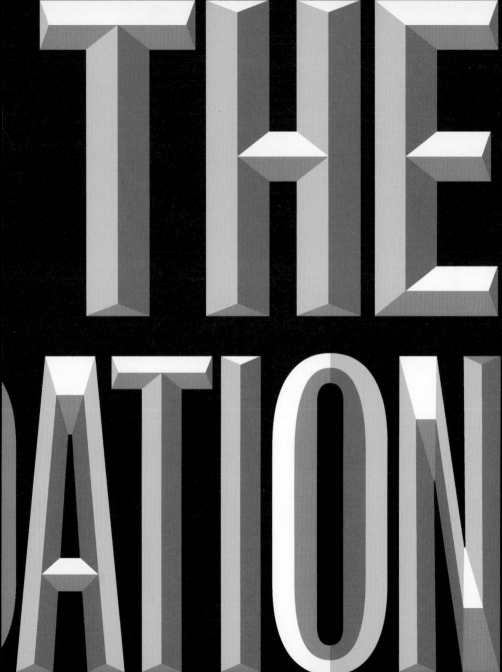

CHAPTER 01

Define Your Priorities

When you're operating at your best and have momentum, often you're pointed at a specific goal. You're stretching yourself and using your valuable skills. Maybe a deadline or timeline is involved. Focus? You've got that too. And usually during these periods, you can quickly assess what else you can take on. Your boundaries are crystal clear.

At least that's how these all-too-rare periods feel for me. I know what I'm doing, when I'm doing it, and how I'm doing it.

How does this happen?

The trick to creating boundaries is creating priorities. The goal comes first. What are you trying to build? Once that is clear in your mind, you're able to draw the blueprint. Those are the boundaries. That is your plan.

This is why it's impossible to stick to our boundaries when our priorities become foggy. Maybe you're the person who's always racing to help someone else before you help yourself. Have you considered where this comes from? Sometimes these patterns are tied to our upbringing, or they're attached to significant relationships or earlier life experiences. Or maybe it's as simple as when a person requests a favor, you get a satisfying zing: *Yes! I can be useful! Let me help!* Like giving advice, it's sometimes easier to help others than it is to help ourselves—or even know how to help ourselves.

But you can usually tell when a favor or request feels like too much, when you're already stretched to your limits or you don't have enough to give. Often, summoning the energy to defend your boundaries is too challenging, and a quick "yes" feels easier to say than a thoughtful "no."

Above all, you must listen to *yourself*. Write down what you want and need on slips of paper and stick them all over your room if you have to—make them impossible to ignore. We so often venture beyond our boundaries because we've lost track of what was important to us. A request arrives or an alert rings and we immediately jump to respond, rather than slowly or thoughtfully assessing whether this is something we can take on.

Let's go big. Can you define the most important priority in your life right now? Maybe it's excelling at your new job, launching a fresh project, building a family, improving your relationship, or making time to relax after a stressful season. There's no wrong answer—and there's no priority that's greater or more important than another. Whatever *you* choose to prioritize is your call.

But consider your number one priority, and the ideal foundation to support it. Maybe you need to find an hour for yourself every day, or you're seeking a new collaborator. Maybe you need to recharge and re-center after running on empty. This foundation will help you flourish.

It's hard to remember our priorities when our boundaries begin to fade, or when we're overwhelmed with other things to do.

Major life events can test even the strongest boundaries. Say you start a job and immediately feel conflicted: You want to prove yourself, but if you say "yes" to unreasonable requests right away, you're indicating your boundaries are flexible or easily broken. That's why boundaries are especially important to consider at the *beginning* of big changes or new relationships. You are setting the stage for your future.

And, look, we all want to be liked. Many of us are conditioned to be kind and amenable. To help and offer support. I don't think I'm the only one who drops four exclamation marks into every email to communicate a sense of being casual and nonconfrontational. Plus, being needed often feels good. Until, of course, it doesn't—when you suddenly find that being accommodating and easygoing can also mean being easily taken advantage of.

You should respect yourself first: your time, your schedule, your life. Respecting yourself is in your control, even if it sometimes might not feel like it. When an opportunity or request comes up, pause and ask yourself, "Does this align with my immediate priority?" rather than defaulting to "Sure! When's best for you?"

A quick caveat: I'm not talking about dodging responsibil-
ities or constantly being defensive. Creating boundaries
doesn't have to come with building enormous, unscalable
walls. Instead, what I want for you—what I want for all of
us—is to understand our own priorities so we're less likely
to find ourselves in undesirable situations.

Your priorities come first. It's not selfish. It's simple.

Carefully draw your own boundaries and you'll feel more
comfortable at work and in your relationships, and you
might even stop second-guessing your conversations or
wondering if someone is mad at you. (They usually aren't,
by the way. And if they are, consider that useful knowledge moving forward.)

Our time is limited. Do you want to spend yours in a clear
and intentional way?

Let's begin defining your priorities—and laying a solid
foundation for your boundaries.

RESPECT YOUR-SELF FIRST

Setting good boundaries starts with self-respect.

Share a few positive qualities about yourself here.

I am:

_____

_____

_____

_____

_____

_____

_____

_____

_____

_____

What is your number one priority right now?

_____

_____

_____

_____

_____

_____

_____

_____

_____

_____

_____

_____

IT'S NOT SELFiSH. IT'S SIMPLE.

Consider the people in your immediate circle (friends, family, coworkers).

Is there anyone on this list who usually doesn't respect your boundaries?

How does that make you feel?

_____

_____

_____

_____

_____

_____

_____

_____

_____

_____

_____

Are you holding on to negative feelings for someone who disappointed you?

Do you think it might feel good to gently let that go?

Write a letter to that person and get out what you need to say.

To: _____

_____

_____

_____

_____

_____

_____

_____

_____

_____

_____

_____

_____

_____

_____

What is something you've been meaning to do but haven't done yet?

What is holding you back?

Do you race to help others before helping yourself?

What is one small way you can move forward with something important to *you* today?

CHAPTER 02

Say No

The email arrived from a friendly writer with a simple question: Would I want to meet for coffee sometime?

Now, I love coffee. And I really love meeting new people. But my initial response to this low-stakes message was a jolt of anxiety. What with returning to working in an office, juggling freelance assignments, and attending my musical theater workshop—not to mention the hours of home-work and new faces I was trying to memorize in all these new settings—my schedule already felt a little too tight. I looked at my calendar to figure out where I could steal a couple of hours, but even thinking about it stressed me out. My life was at capacity.

Yet in the moment I still felt compelled to respond, "Would love to! When's good for you?" We do this often because finding the right words to draw boundaries is never easy. It can feel like you're letting someone down, or pretending you're so terribly important that you don't have time to spare.

But you must listen to your gut instinct. Offering a hes-itant and disingenuous "yes" is so much worse than a clear and definitive "no." Because a wishy-washy "yes" is loaded with baggage. When you're stressed and your inbox is a graveyard of unopened messages, yet you're pulling yourself away to go to that coffee, you're going to wonder why you didn't simply say "no" to begin with. I understand this might sound silly. A fun social meeting is a minor occasion for setting some boundaries, but practicing with these smaller concerns can help you navigate larger issues.

If your initial reaction to a request or invitation is to feel stressed or overwhelmed, consider it a clue. If you can't decide whether to move forward, take that as another clue. These are the seeds of a "no" if you're brave enough to see them—and then able to find the right words to act on them.

When it comes to an opportunity, job, gig, or something as simple as grabbing coffee, we often know the answer we would like to give. If it's not an immediate *yes*, we usually want to say *no*. But instead of being direct, we default to avoiding, ignoring, hiding, ghosting or, of course, saying, "Yeah, maybe," while hoping the other person will forget, hoping *they'll* reschedule.

I didn't meet up for that coffee, by the way. I told the writer I was sorry, but I was too swamped and suggested we chat on the phone at some point. Guess what? Nothing bad happened. Four years later, we're actually friends, and she recently told me my response had inspired her—she respected how I protected my time. Little did she know I debated writing that short email back to her for hours. It wasn't easy to write. It never is. And yet everything worked out. I didn't burn any bridges. All was well.

There are, of course, plenty of ways to say no. There's the definitive, shut-it-down *no, I can't*. The *no* with caveats (such as, "Check in with me a little bit later," which often just delays the answer you already know you want to give). There's the *no* with a hedge ("I'll try to come by if you're still out!") and the *no* with an elaborate explanation ("I'm so sorry and would totally love to be there and feel really terrible please don't hate me but . . ."). And on and on.

But, typically, you don't need all of that. Just like you, most people have also said *no* and understand that time is precious. It's not an affront to them, a signal that you don't like or care about them. It's simply a sign that you value your own time and energy.

Remember that for every instance you have anxiety about saying no, the person on the other end has been in your position before, too. Don't cloud your thinking by labeling a *yes* as you being "good" or a *no* as you being "bad." Your boundaries reflect decisions, not designations of self-worth. You're communicating to someone else who is making exactly the same calculations with their own days, schedules, and commitments. If they can't handle your decision, that's on them.

Here are a few examples about how to say *no*. Add, edit, and expand to make them relevant to your own life. Resist fluffing up your responses. Start small. Just be honest. Your boundaries are important—don't gloss over them.

- To a casual acquaintance, who wants to get together: *I'm sorry I can't this weekend. I hope you have a great time!*

- To your boss, who is piling work on you: *I don't think I'll be able to complete this by the deadline. Can we discuss the best way to move forward?*

- To the stranger asking for advice: *I'd like to help, but I'm spinning too many plates and won't be able to offer anything substantive right now.*

If you can, try not to fib. Dropping a white lie into an email or text has the tendency to come back and get you. For instance, you say you can't make it to your friend's show because you're out of town . . . then you run into them at brunch the next day. Let's all avoid that specific brand of awkwardness by not offering fake excuses in the first place.

Besides, you don't need to lie about your boundaries. Respect them. Clear communication helps you draw those lines. It begins by being honest with yourself about what you want to do (or don't want to do), how you wish to spend your time, and which events or moments draw you in and make you excited to see them through. Those deserve your most enthusiastic *yes*.

Showing up when and where you truly want to show up—and with your total commitment—is the goal.

Are you ready to practice saying *no*?

Who do you find it hard to say *no* to?

Why do you think it's so difficult?

_____

_____

_____

_____

_____

_____

_____

_____

_____

_____

_____

_____

SAY NO WHEN IT'S A NO

Are you putting something off because you're avoiding confrontation?

Describe the situation here.

_____

_____

_____

_____

_____

_____

_____

_____

_____

_____

Our habits create behavior.

Think about an event that you always say *yes* to, but which you aren't feeling excited about now.

What would you like to say or do instead?

_____

_____

_____

_____

_____

_____

_____

_____

_____

_____

_____

_____

_____

Let's get down to basics:

I want

_____

_____

I do not want

_____

_____

I want

_____

_____

I do not want

_____

_____

I want

_____

_____

I do not want

_____

_____

Write down a
moment where you
protected your time
or your space. What
happened?

**What did you learn (about
yourself or someone else)?**

Your present self loves to say *yes*. (It feels easier!)

But what would your future self want you to say?

BE KiND TO YOUR FUTURE SELF

CHAPTER 03

Claiming Space

Lemurs don't listen.

They may have perfectly round, expressive eyes, puffy fur, and wonderfully striped tails—at least my favorite species, the ring-tailed lemurs, do. But they really don't like to listen, especially when it comes to setting boundaries.

A few summers ago, I traveled to the Duke Lemur Center in Durham, North Carolina, where hundreds of lemurs live in and around a lush, one hundred-acre forest. When I heard visitors could go on a walk through the woods tour with the cute creatures, I thought: *Sign me up.*

There was one primary rule: Always keep a three-foot distance from the lemurs. We humans had to stay away because "the lemurs don't always respect that boundary," joked the animal keepers.

But they were right. As we made our way through the forest, one lemur darted in front of me, while another dashed ahead to grab some snacks. As we walked, the lemurs often jumped only inches away. Every time a lemur came too close, I froze. I didn't want to break the boundary—the lemur rule—even if they did as they pleased.

Sometimes boundaries just don't stick. We're pushing past someone else's line. Or we're trying to follow our own rules, no matter how tempting it is to break them.

As the lemurs ran and jumped, repeatedly wiping out the three-foot rule, I could only think that there's no fighting nature. If lemurs won't listen, at least we can continue to create and maintain our *own* boundaries.

Always keep a three-foot distance. There's a clear and distinct rule.

What would an equally clear rule look like in your own life? How would that change the structure of your work, your relationships, or what you accept or decline? What does a metaphorical or symbolic three-foot distance look like to you? Because a few feet is both a lot of space—and not much at all. It's enough for you to draw a perimeter and protect your personal zone, while continuing to view your surroundings.

Of course, our own boundaries get a little amorphous or complicated. So how can we determine our own distances at work, or in a personal project, or even with ourselves?

We can begin by starting from scratch. Yes, really. Make something up. You're already drawing your lines, considering your priorities, and saying *no*. Now let's sketch some rough boundaries and see how they feel.

When it comes to your professional life, which rules feel vital to your success *and* happiness? Maybe your coworker has a habit of messaging you at 8 A.M., even though your workday technically doesn't start for another two hours. You usually respond, further feeding this cycle of behavior. Your new rule could be to respond only during work hours or, even better, during a specific timeframe when you're able to fully concentrate. That might feel impossible in the beginning. The idea of wanting to be "available" often blurs our boundaries.

Before going forward, ask yourself, *What am I taking away from myself in order to give to someone else?* Because if you don't protect yourself first, you'll be left with less to give.

It's easy for boundaries to blur during random daily interactions. Let's say you're running out the door to meet someone. Your commute is timed down to the minute and everything's on track. But as you turn the corner, you bump into your chattiest colleague and get caught up in conversation. You don't want to be rude. Yet instead of saying, "I have to meet a friend, but let's catch up later!" you derail your own plan. Fifteen minutes later, as you're leaving, cue the negative self-talk: *I know what I needed to do. Why couldn't I just do it?*

These blips in our day are subtle forms of people-pleasing. Except . . . you're not actually pleasing, you're only *appeasing* the part of yourself that wants to be considered "good" and "nice." In the end, you diminish your priorities and affirm that your needs are less important than someone else's needs.

To be clear: There's nothing wrong with being nice! But this is one example of the tricky ways in which we often sacrifice our boundaries, even without realizing it.

Say, for instance, you're out to dinner with friends and the talk turns gossipy and a little mean. You're sensing this conversation doesn't feel good or productive. Besides, you actually like the person they're all chatting about now. And yet something strange happens: You chime in anyway, throwing in a little dig because what's the harm, right?

These informal conversational boundaries are everywhere. They're present in what you want to share or don't want to, what you want to rehash or would rather not. It's hard to draw these lines in the moment, but when you don't, you leave feeling misaligned or uncomfortable. There is no harm—and a lot of power—in changing the subject or saying, "Let's talk about something else." In fact, doesn't that feel sort of freeing?

Sometimes drawing a line around what you aren't OK with is more about what you do rather than what you say. Actions outweigh emotional reactions. When your boss sends an email on a Sunday, or an acquaintance starts overstepping, or a parent turns your phone call in a negative direction, remember that you can't control someone else, but you can control your own response.

Define your space and maintain your three-foot rule.

Stay true to what you choose to do, no matter what someone else might want you to do.

DESIGN YOUR DAY, DESIGN YOUR LIFE.

Plan out your day here.

What must happen for you to call it a successful day?

_____

_____

_____

_____

_____

_____

_____

_____

_____

_____

_____

_____

Think about a
recent interaction
that made you feel
slightly worse after
it was over.

**What would you do
differently next time?**

Do you want to create some new space in your schedule?

Consider the week ahead. What do you want to add?

What do you want to eliminate?

Let's play with conversational boundaries.

Pretend you're trapped in a chat you want to get out of.

What are three ways for you to change the subject or remove yourself entirely?

1.

2.

3.

Define one of your new, unbreakable three-foot rules.

What line will you not allow someone else to cross?

When did you last
feel like someone
was taking advantage
of your time, energy,
or talent?

How did you react?

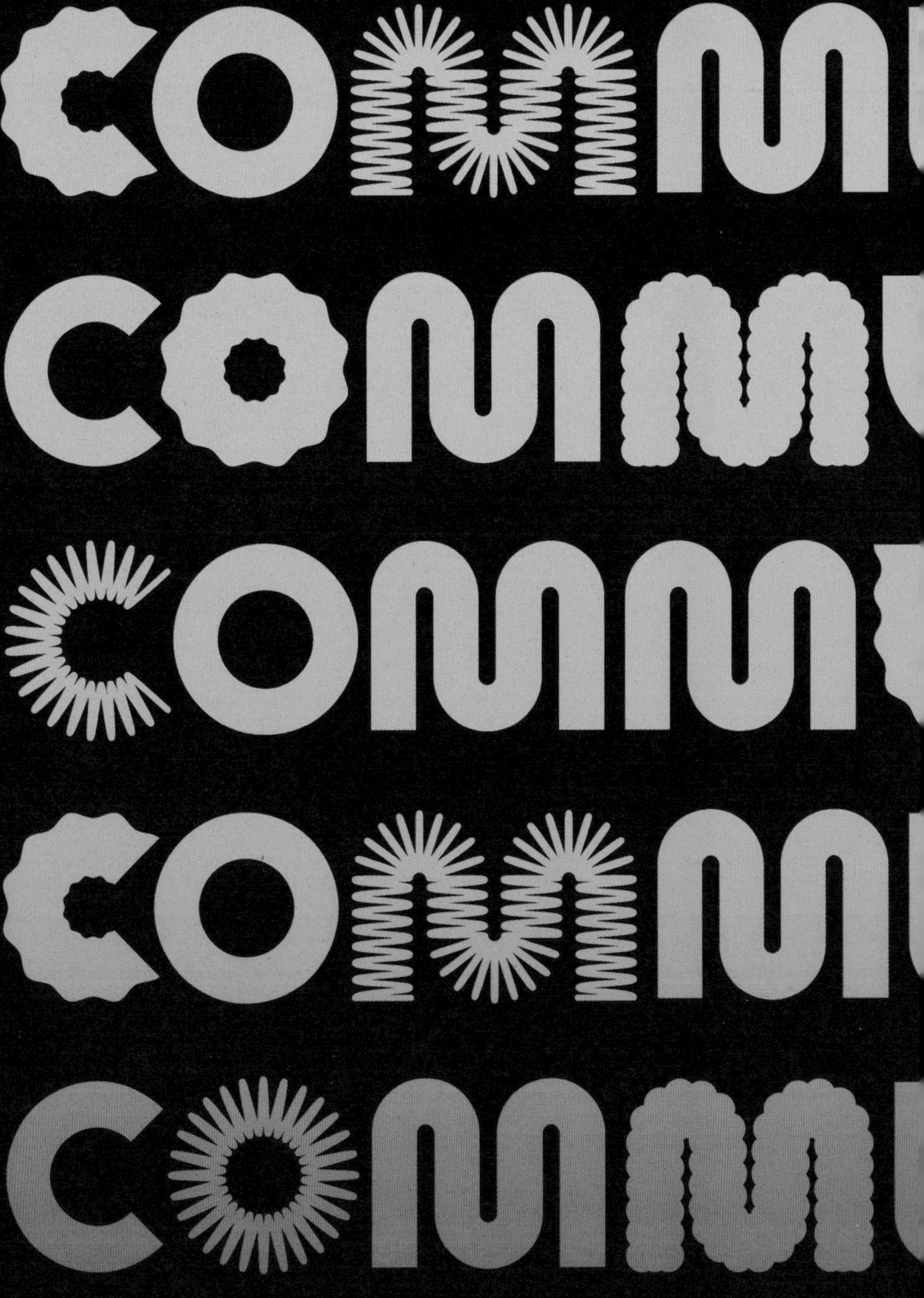

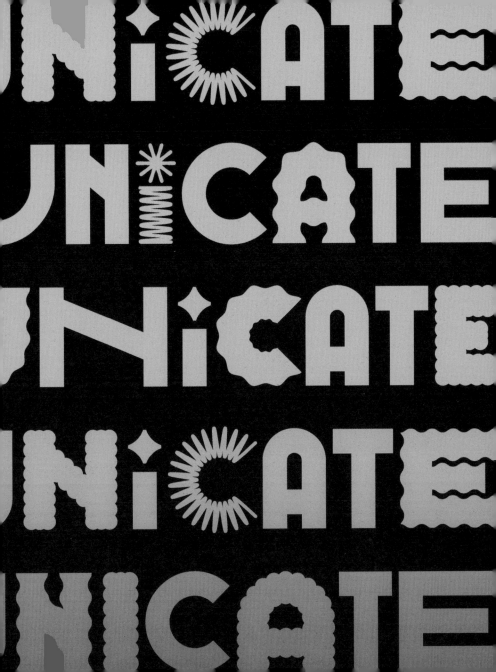

CHAPTER 04

Flake with Grace

You RSVPed two months ago and now you're looking for a way out. This wasn't the best week, and the last thing you want to do is attend a conference with strangers. What do you do?

If you're like me, you might hit the avoidance button. You think if you wait long enough, it'll simply take care of itself. Or, better yet, disappear.

We both know that's not going to happen. You eventually must make the decision, and putting it off only makes it worse. Sometimes you have to flake—or, as we'll call it, *flake gracefully*. As a solution, you're going to draw some fresh boundaries, or create some new ones that never existed.

The need to bow out gracefully happens more than you think. We overcommit and misjudge our future selves. Surely, the me of ten days or six months from now will have more time, energy, or desire to attend that party, write that article, meet for that play group. But, inevitably, the date starts creeping up and you're desperate for an alternative. Good news: There's time. You can still flake if you do it with grace. Flake with dignity. Flake with a smile and get yourself out of the situation. Even better news: If you can master flaking gracefully, you'll never have to ghost somebody again.

Flaking doesn't have to be terrible. In fact, if you do it right, it can be a gift.

***

Oh, sorry, just saw this! Still going to try to swing by tonight.

Look familiar? Sometimes these words might be true—your phone was on silent or you were having a deep talk with your best friend—but in most scenarios we lean on these crutches because we think they'll make the other person feel better. Harmless, supposedly, but when they're actually not true, we're lying about our priorities and our boundaries.

Why lie? You can respond with the truth. Instead try saying one of the following:

- *I'd like to be there, but I have another commitment.*

- *I was looking forward to seeing you, but I could use a night in to recharge.*

- *I can't jump on the phone today, but let's talk next week.*

Simple, easy, clear.

When you start a relationship by letting people invade your boundaries, it becomes even more tempting later to ghost or flake at the last minute, which only makes *you* feel worse. The alternative, however, is to be honest. You stick to what you're going to do—or don't. If you don't want to go somewhere, don't go. If you don't want to do something, don't do it. But do not hesitate.

The golden rule to flaking is this: *Communicate quickly and with clarity.* That's it.

If you can't follow through on a commitment, fire off the text and get yourself out of the situation. Trust me, it won't get any easier the more time passes. You will feel infinitely better, lighter, and happier with a clean slate and clear head. You'll eliminate the dread making you feel antsy or guilty or anxious.

I won't be able to _____ **because** _____ .

That's all you have to say. Really!

- *I won't be able to make it out this weekend because money's a little tight right now.*

- *I won't be able to complete my story by the deadline because I have additional research to do.*

- *I won't be able to call tonight because I need to work on a project for tomorrow.*

You can say that you're sorry. And you can offer as much or little explanation as you want. Your reasons are your reasons. Most people will understand. And if they don't, that's helpful information, too. Respecting boundaries is just as important as being able to define them. People rarely get mad if you bow out early, or provide an update about the situation. But if you disappear, the person on the other end starts to wonder what's going on and spins a story in their head. Silence is the enemy. No one likes to be ignored.

Now is the time to bow out. When you do, you're letting the other person out of an obligation too, freeing them to spend their time in a different way. It can be an act of kindness to cancel. Seriously. Consider the energy you bring to an event or meeting where you wish you were somewhere else. You might feel annoyed or checked out. Trust your gut and do what you want to do. Show up where you want to show up.

But I have obligations! I can't flake on my quarterly review with my boss or hide away like a hermit.

I get it. Many obligations feel etched in stone. When you're unable to flake, embrace your boundaries instead. Maybe you can't cancel, but you can create some guardrails.

When there's no way to avoid dinner with the family friend who somehow always makes you feel bad about yourself, you can still decline after-dinner drinks:

That's a nice idea but I'm going to have to call it a night!

And then you leave.

It might feel awkward at first, especially if you're new to drawing these lines. Persist anyway. A few uncomfortable moments are still better than betraying the borders you want to keep, the ones that are important to you.

Practice drawing your lines and flaking gracefully.

You will feel better—and more like yourself—by honoring your boundaries.

Do you feel overcommitted at the moment?

Among your obligations, which ones excite you, and which ones ignite a sense of dread?

When is the last time you flaked on something?

How did it make you feel?

And when did *you* last get flaked on?
How did it make you feel?

Write a message to someone explaining why you're unable to do "that thing," whatever it is.

What would happen if you sent it?

_____

_____

_____

_____

_____

_____

_____

_____

_____

_____

_____

_____

_____

_____

Who in your life is consistently good at keeping their boundaries?

What could you learn from watching them?

SIMPLE
EASY
CLEAR

CONTROL YOUR CALENDAR

Can you change your plans?

List three upcoming obligations—and alternatives that would make them feel easier to manage.

My Plans

1.
_____

_____

2.
_____

_____

3.
_____

_____

My Alternatives

1.
_____

_____

2.
_____

_____

3.
_____

_____

Fill in the blanks with whatever you need right now:

I won't be able to _____

because _____.

How does that make
you feel?

TAKE THE PRESSURE

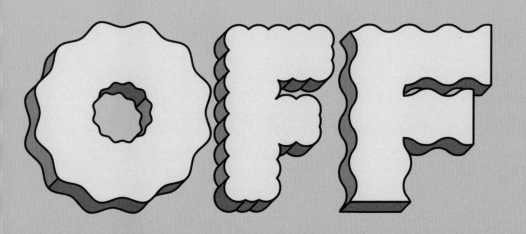

KEEP THE PROMISES YOU MAKE TO YOUR-SELF

Sometimes the promises we make to ourselves are the most important ones.

What is one new commitment you'd like to keep for yourself?

Outline how you plan to do that here.

I will:

_____

_____

_____

_____

_____

_____

_____

_____

_____

_____

_____

_____

CHAPTER 05

Make It Easy

How much clarity do you have about today?

Is your day planned down to the minute, or feeling loose and flexible? Do you know when your workday will start and when it might end? Do you have time scheduled for the events, people, and projects that are meaningful to you? Is your attitude "Let's see what happens," or "Here are my top three goals for the day"?

If you enter the day unsure of your intentions, you—and your boundaries—are vulnerable.

You can't uphold a boundary if you haven't defined it yet. And you can't define it if you're distracted, scattered, or reaching for your phone every three minutes. (I've tried.) It's obvious that we live in a fast-paced world operating at a frenetic pace: Do this, finish that, go there, reply now. But you don't have to live that way if it doesn't serve you. Or at least not all the time. One of your boundaries— perhaps the most important boundary—is to make things easy on yourself.

Imagine moving seamlessly among commitments. You know where you're going, what you have to give, and you are able to honor your own needs while recognizing and valuing everyone else's. There's less "What am I supposed to be doing?" and more "This is exactly what I'm doing." You slide past distractions with skill, and you've already declined activities you were dreading. Sound daunting? It doesn't have to be.

How do you feel after conquering your laundry pile, clearing away junk, and straightening up your workspace? Better, right? Staying organized can carry you through obstacles until you're on the other side.

A similar pattern happens when you're working on a project or collaborating with other people. Clarity will help the entire process. Some early questions to ask:

- Have you decided when, where, and how often you're going to meet?

- What is your system for storing and sharing information with each other?

- Will you enter a meeting frazzled or with optimism about the work ahead?

These small choices create ripple effects for the rest of your relationship, and the project itself. How you handle the small things influences how you handle the big things.

The first step to making it easy on yourself is to do a survey of your surroundings. Is your desktop cluttered? Is your calendar a mess? Are a bunch of tiny to-dos hanging over your head? Now it's time to clean it up. The goal is to scrub away all the small bits of friction or distraction. Keep a clear mind and your boundaries will become clear.

If this seems overwhelming, start with the smallest possible step. Take everything rattling around your brain and put it into a list. Every project you need to complete, every errand you need to run, every commitment you want to keep. Getting things out of your head and onto paper or a note in your phone creates an instant boundary. Now these things exist outside of you. They don't have to occupy valuable space in your daily thoughts.

Once you have your list, it's time to ask the crucial question: What do I need to make each item *easy*?

For example, if you want to exercise more often, do you need to pump your bike tires? You want to be able to simply jump on the bike and go.

Or maybe you've been saying you want to throw monthly dinner parties but are too bogged down by the details. (Place settings! Guest list! Everyone's so busy anyway!) Sometimes things don't have to be so hard. You can break down every element into easy tasks. For instance, look at your calendar and pick a date. (Instant boundary.) Then make a list of people you want to invite. Send them a note, and keep moving forward.

We can get so worked up and distracted by fictional possible *outcomes* that we fail to begin.

While these small steps may not seem exciting, there is a big payoff. You spend less energy searching for *what* to do and don't have to work as hard on the things you *want* to do. Creating something new, succeeding at work, and maintaining relationships shouldn't be so difficult, should it? Yet without structure, everything requires extra effort.

Disclaimer: I'm not super organized in the traditional sense. Ask me to make a budget and I'll run away screaming. Assign me to manage a team calendar and I'll say, "Thanks, but no." And yet, when I put small efforts toward creating structure, whether that's through writing lists or planning my day, I feel calmer and like I'm respecting my boundaries. And when you feel that ease and connection, you find progress.

Simply put, cutting out distractions allows you to find the deep focus necessary for the things that matter to you. You're choosing what is important, not getting sidetracked by interruptions.

When you're organizing and clarifying your life, one question to ask yourself is, "Does this make my boundaries *easier* or *harder* to maintain?"

Look at your surroundings, habits, and patterns.

Ask the question, clear away the clutter, and make your next move easy.

Would you describe yourself as an organized person?

Tell me about one method you use to coordinate your life.

Time for a little creative sprint.

Consider this page your most important priority for the next five minutes.

Write down everything on your mind right now.

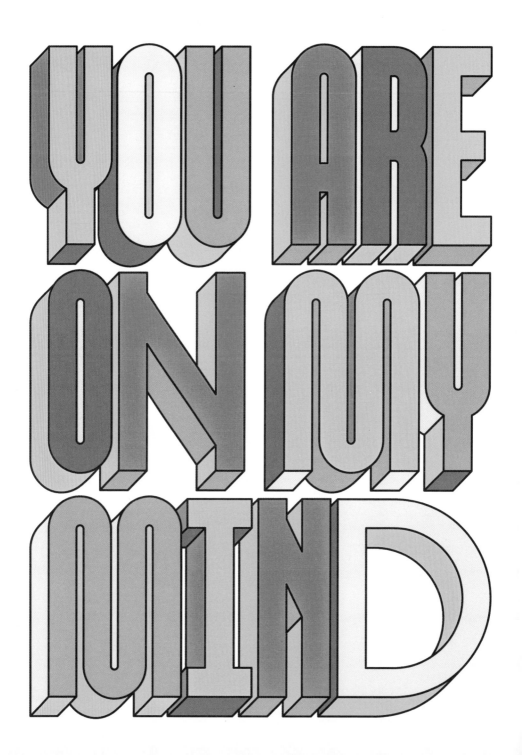

What is one plan, event, or task you've been meaning to do but have been putting off?

Break it down into easy steps here.

- _____

- _____

- _____

- _____

- _____

- _____

- _____

- _____

- _____

Track distractions
as they arise today.
Group them under
the following
categories.

Distractions I have control over:

_____

_____

_____

_____

_____

_____

_____

_____

_____

Distractions I do not have control over:

_____

_____

_____

_____

_____

_____

_____

_____

_____

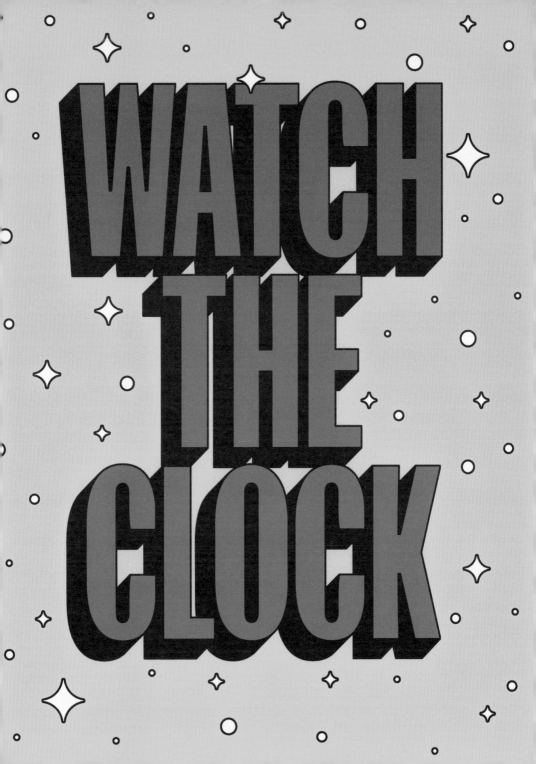

When is the last time you felt a deep focus on what you were doing?

Write about where you were, who you were with, and the kind of environment you were in.

Can you re-create that focus today?

It's hard to embrace boundaries if you don't define them.

Sketch an outline of your plans for the rest of your day (or for tomorrow).

8 A.M. _____

9 A.M. _____

10 A.M. _____

11 A.M. _____

12 P.M. _____

1 P.M. _____

2 P.M. _____

3 P.M. _____

4 P.M. _____

5 P.M. _____

6 P.M. _____

7 P.M. _____

8 P.M. _____

9 P.M. _____

KEEP **YOUR** SPACE CLEAN, KEEP YOUR MiND CLEAR

Think back to the
most important
priority you declared
earlier in this journal.

**Do you have any systems in
place around that priority?**

What is one routine or habit that would help you take a positive step forward?

CHAPTER 06

The Art of Asking

You need help. This isn't an accusation. I'm not saying you can't do it all on your own. (You can try, and I'm guessing you already have.) But wouldn't it be nice—useful, clarifying, boosting—to get some encouragement or wisdom from someone who might know more than you?

We all need help. And if you're similar to me, you probably hate asking for it. Do you find yourself exhausting every other option first before opening your mouth? Why? Usually it's because you want to avoid inconveniencing people or creating a sense of obligation. You don't want to be a burden.

This happens all the time in our personal and professional lives. We know it might turbocharge our work to find an accountability partner but don't want to bug someone. Or we need more information about a job or project but don't want to look insecure. Asking is simple—but often scary.

For years, I put off applying for graduate school because the application required a letter of recommendation. *No one wants to write these things,* I said to myself. *I don't want to be a bother.* But my own dreams were in a holding pattern because I couldn't send an email. One email!

I finally asked for help. A former colleague replied immediately and wrote the nicest and most affirming letter. This didn't only complete my application, but it gave me more confidence in my path until that moment. All that, from a short email with a small request.

When drawing boundaries in our lives, we're getting clarity on how we want to spend our time and where we want to go. This creates a cascading effect. You want to *keep* growing. One hitch: Steps for growth often require asking for help. This involves venturing beyond our safe borders into an unknown world of vulnerability and possible rejection. Asking for help often feels like an embarrassing admission. *Nope, I don't have all the answers. Yes, I need you to help me find them.*

We can reframe those feelings. You're not asking for help. You're letting people in. You're allowing someone else into your process—whatever that process looks like for you.

The idea of letting someone in already feels less stressful, doesn't it? It sounds like partnering up on a plan. You're not nudging or inconveniencing. Maybe you're actually giving another person an opportunity to feel useful.

And when you feel good about the ask, there's nothing to worry about. The primary step to feeling good about the ask is to make it as clear as you can. Here are some questions to consider before you begin:

- *Who are you asking?* Find the person you suspect will have the best possible answer for you. Make a long list of people if you'd like—but then start with one.

- *What is the time commitment?* Are you asking someone for an hour-long interview over Zoom, or to meet you for lunch (which always take three hours no matter what)?

When you're clear on your end, the other person can evaluate and respect their own boundaries, and get back to you with a quicker *yes* or *no*.

- *Specifically when does this need to happen?* Ask early and be honest about deadlines. Consider how *you* would want to be approached with a similar request. Are you likely to give your full attention to an email arriving on a Friday afternoon, or would you be better able to concentrate on a Tuesday morning?

- *Where does this need to happen?* Do you have to meet for coffee, or are you defaulting to that because it's the norm? Think about whether you can make the response easier on the other person. What location would make this more convenient for them?

- *Why are you asking—what do you hope to learn or achieve?* This requires some precautionary thinking on your part. Sometimes we think we want to ask for something, but what we really want is affirmation—for the person on the other end to say, "Keep going." Is that your intention? If so, tell the other person what you need. Or consider whether you can give yourself the encouragement you're seeking.

- *How will this benefit both of you?* Maybe the person you're asking will teach you something new, or maybe you can help them with something later. When you consider asking as a new possibility for connection or growth, it becomes much less intimidating. Perhaps you'll soon be able to pass that knowledge or help on to someone else.

The *who, what, when, where, why,* and *how* questions focus you before you reach out. Remember that if your intention is unclear from the beginning, you're more likely to receive cloudy advice.

This shouldn't be exhausting, by the way. Do this enough times and it will feel easy and natural. You can also pose your request in whatever way feels most honest and authentic to you.

Also, when you feel the urge to "pick someone's brain" over coffee, go back to the question, What do you *actually* want to know? If you want to learn about a company's hiring practice, or how to level up your writing career, then you have specific questions—don't be afraid to ask them. Being clear and direct will respect the person's boundaries at the same time you're respecting your own.

Give a gift to yourself: Make a promise to ask for one thing today—whatever that one thing is you need right now.

Maybe you'll contact the friend who said he'd read your book proposal, or ask your boss about taking next Friday off, or follow up on that time-sensitive request you made a month ago.

Focus, be brave, and ask.

YOU FEEL GOOD ABOUT THE ASK

How does asking for a favor make you feel?

And how do you feel when someone asks you for a favor?

Whose help do you need right now?

List five people who might be able to offer you advice, inspiration, or support.

Circle one person you would like to contact today.

1. _____

2. _____

3. _____

4. _____

5. _____

Think back to the
last time you asked
someone for their
support.

How did they respond?

Write down the worst thing that could happen if you asked for help.

Can you handle it? I bet you can.

Who in your life could use a hand right now?

List a few simple ways you might be able to offer assistance.

_____

_____

_____

_____

_____

_____

_____

_____

_____

_____

_____

_____

RETHINK

REFRAME

HOW ARE YOU?

Try the who, what, when, where, why, and how approach to asking.

Fill in the blanks in the following letter with what you need.

Hi, _____. I was wondering if you could help me with

something. I'm in the middle of _____ and would

like some advice regarding _____. Would you

have ____ minutes to talk on the phone within the next ____ weeks

so I could ask you a few questions about your experience? I can

also send over some questions if that's easier. Thank you so much.

Imagine a good friend asks you for help this week.

How can you respond in a way that respects your boundaries but also feels honest and true to you?

What's one thing you can ask for today?

(Don't worry, it can be a small ask.)

When will you do it?

TOP
SEC

CHAPTER 07

How to Rest

A two-week vacation. A calendar with acres of empty days. Zoning out in front of your favorite show.

What does rest look like to you? The *to you* perspective is essential, because rest looks very different to different people. Extroverts might feel recharged after a late night out with a group, while an introvert may seek the solitude of a peaceful morning. How do you like to rest? More importantly, *when* do you rest?

Here's one habit I'm trying to change: I'll put off taking a break because I feel like I haven't earned it. You might recognize that impulse, the mistaken belief that you need to completely drain yourself to zero in order to start building yourself back up again—that rest isn't crucial unless it's hard-won.

But there's a problem with this strategy. When you put off resting until you absolutely need it, you're resting because it's critical, not restorative. Instead, you create a cycle of "until I fulfill this random goal, I don't deserve to relax." And when you're not recharging yourself, your defenses fall, your habits go haywire and—surprise!—your boundaries are ineffective.

When you're well-rested, it's easier to do things, including respecting your boundaries. Slowing down is necessary, especially when you're overwhelmed. Doing more and doing it faster isn't the recipe to "fixing" what's wrong. Taking a step back and reconnecting to your original intention is the better solution.

It can be especially difficult to rest when other people depend on you and you're trying to fill multiple roles— the model employee or student, the perfect mother or always available uncle, the wise counsel for friends— all while maintaining the perfect portrait of health and well-being for yourself.

Without rest, you begin to scatter everywhere. You need to remember that your primary job is to keep *yourself* clearheaded and capable. You can't be useful to anyone, much less yourself, if you're not recharged. So how do you get there?

Let's look at your surroundings, feelings, and energy.

People often feel fired up and newly in control of their lives during vacation. Abandoning daily routines and embracing a new city, schedule, and breakfast buffet urge adaptation. Instead of cycling through your usual activities, you begin to ask, "What do I actually like and want to do?" Typically, you carry this question home.

But hopping on a plane isn't the only way to hit the reset button. Start by observing your daily surroundings—and shaking them up. For example, if you spend most of your day at a desk, walking to a fresh spot could help you feel more awake and curious. On a larger scale, if you're feeling stagnant at home, you could rearrange furniture, give away items you no longer need, or even consider moving. (To be fair, moving is definitely not a restful activity, but being happier where you live can improve your life over the long term.)

If you're feeling tired, overworked, or overwhelmed, try to unravel your feelings into two possible needs: physical rest or emotional rest. If you've been training for a 5K or haven't had a night off in weeks, your body might require a break. But if you recently had a fight with your partner or are dealing with a troubling work situation, your brain might need the break. Pinpointing your specific flavor of tiredness can make a difference. I can't tell you how many times I've told myself I should implode a project or get a new job when all I really needed was to go to sleep by 10 P.M. for once in my life.

You can also consider the energy sources around you. Sometimes we become drained by an activity that previously gave us a boost. This is OK! It happens. But you don't have to passively continue doing what you've always done. Metaphorically pull the plug. Which energy sources are you allowing into your life? Social media, events, personal obligations, work commitments, creative projects? Which power you up and which make you want to sleep for a decade?

You might need a rest that's the opposite of your energy sources. If you're overstimulated by external events and nighttime obligations, can you set aside one night a week dedicated to yourself? If you're feeling burdened by always being the initiator in a friendship, can you ask your friend if they'll plan your next group outing?

Sometimes, too, we find ourselves in periods of intense action and change and very little downtime. This is inevitable. But as I've often found, you can get through practically anything if there's a deadline or an end date. Perhaps you can't build a lot of rest into your daily routine now, but can you pinpoint the moment when your activity level is going to shift even just a bit? Maybe it's after the holidays, or next semester, or once you've settled in after a big move, or following a busy work season. Whatever it is, hold it tight. Choose a rest date, put it on your calendar, and move forward knowing most things don't last forever, and you deserve some time for yourself.

Giving yourself a break is another boundary to create and respect.

Don't feel guilty over what you can't do now. Clarify what you need, and then do what you can.

Rest serves you—and everyone around you.

Consider whether
you need more
silence (think naps
and meditation)
or more stimuli
(think podcasts
and people).

Write down what you need.

During stressful or overwhelmed moments, what helps you relax?

Think about people, places, movement, actions, and activities.

Where do you spend most of your time?

What is the opposite of those surroundings?

_____

_____

_____

_____

_____

_____

_____

_____

_____

_____

You can fire off a text anytime, but it takes deliberate effort to schedule a long catch-up with a friend.

Is there anyone you want to connect with who you haven't spoken to in a while?

What would you share?

_____

_____

_____

_____

_____

_____

_____

_____

_____

_____

What's the last great thing (article, book, or something else) that you read?

Describe why it inspired you.

What does the most calm and well-rested version of you look like?

Plan your dream
vacation, from your
ideal location to
how you'd spend
each day.

There are no limits.

Where I would go:

_____

_____

_____

_____

_____

_____

_____

_____

_____

What I would do:

_____

_____

_____

_____

_____

_____

_____

_____

_____

REST SER- VES YOU

MY BOUNDARIES

ARE MY

BELIEFS

How can you keep strong boundaries while resting?

For example, turning off your phone, blocking off time, planning a solo outing.

What feels right to you?

THE
FIN

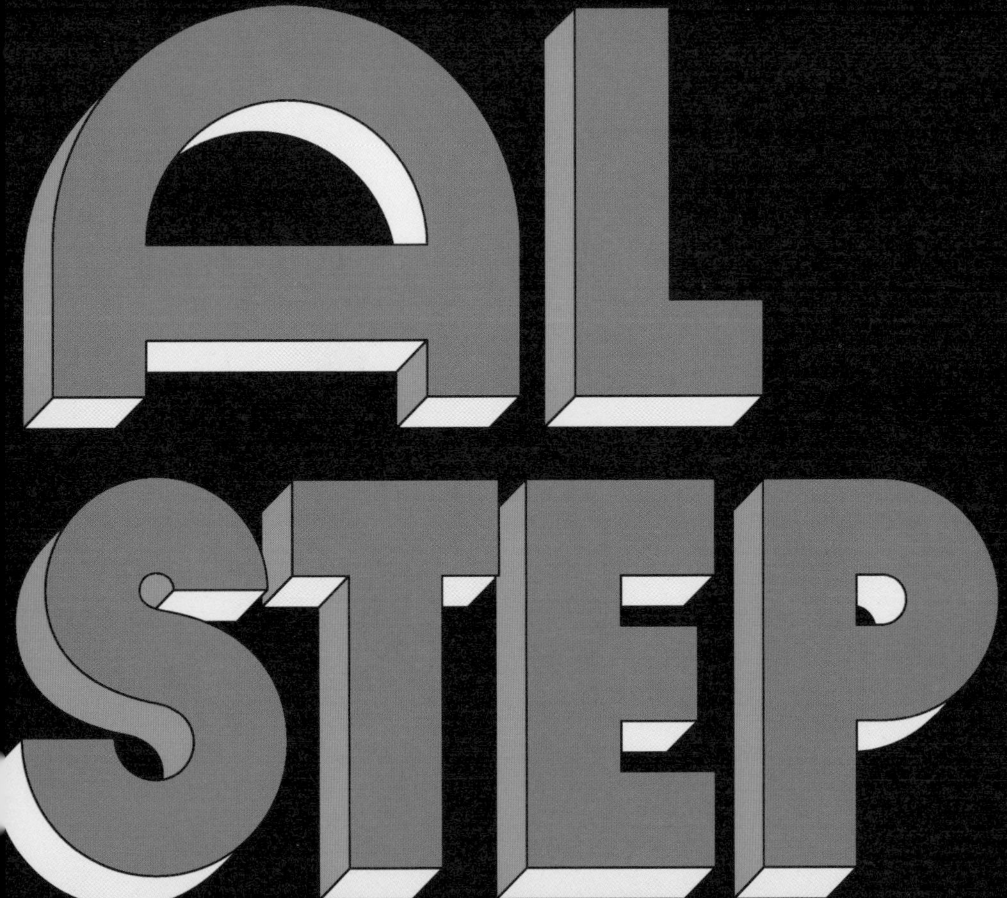
AL
STEP

CHAPTER 08

Do It (or Don't)

You're confident. You're ready. You know what you want.

Equally as important, you know what you _don't_ want.

There are two options: _doing_ and _not doing_. Everything else is the messy middle. It may sound like a joke, but now you understand it really is that simple. I'm a frequent visitor to that middle ground, and you might be, too. It's where boundaries are at their fuzziest, indecision reigns, and you feel like a "well, I don't know, maybe" sponge. But when you commit to doing (or not doing, the _no_ is as crucial as the _yes_), everything becomes less complicated. Your foundation is solid. And your boundaries? They are unshakable in the best possible way.

There's a lot of danger in pausing when you're just getting started defining your boundaries. There's also a risk in adapting your needs to everyone else's before you clarify your own.

You know what you want to do. Be clear with your words and intentions. Draw lines where you previously never imagined them. Forget what was and what could be and look at what is now. Creating and respecting boundaries isn't always going to be easy, but it will get easier the more you do it.

Here is how to practice:

- Say "yes" only when you want to say _yes_. And say "no" when you want to say _no_.

- Redraw your boundaries whenever you need to—whether that's daily, weekly, or yearly.

- Find your confidence even when you feel unsure.

- Define the time and space you need to do your best work.

- Forgive yourself when things don't go perfectly the first (or the second) time.

- Always, without fail, try again.

When you begin to live with clarity, respecting your own boundaries and the boundaries of others, get ready. People will notice. They might want to nudge you off course. Or they might want to know your secret.

Their reactions don't matter either way. You are living the way you want to live. No one is walking all over you; you're not making yourself small to suit someone else. You're not being talked into doing something you don't want to do.

What do your boundaries feel like?

You work when you say you're going to work. You rest when you say you're going to rest. You offer what you can offer—no more and no less. You're people-pleasing exactly one person: yourself.

Advocating for yourself and being conscientious aren't mutually exclusive. In fact, they can serve each other.

I can see all the work I still have to do—and will continue to do—regarding setting boundaries. You might see the same in yourself: Moments you were nudged into making a decision. Lingering resentment because you didn't let yourself speak up. Feeling uncomfortable or like the odd person out. Those moments occur when your actions aren't aligned with your intentions, and your boundaries are more susceptible to being broken.

But you do know how to act. Most of the time, you do know what you want to do, but you may be too nervous or intimidated to speak your mind.

Speak up anyway. This is your one life.

I wish you fewer moments of debating your choices and more moments of getting what you desire.

I wish you clarity and bold boundary lines.

Most of all, I wish you would do it—or don't.

The future, as always, is yours.

YOU
KNOW
WHAT
YOU
WANT

Fill in the blanks:

I will do _____

_____

_____

_____.

I will not do _____

_____

_____

_____.

If you're feeling burnt out, imagine what lighting a new flame would do.

Describe the energy you want yourself to have.

When have you experienced a messy middle?

How did you get out of it?

DESIGN THE LIFE YOU WANT TO LIVE

Imagine it is one year from today.

What do you hope you have achieved?

What is one space where you feel confident?

What is one space where you feel insecure?

Try to unravel why you feel that way.

YOU ARE CONFI-DENT. YOU ARE STR-ONG.

How have you held firm to a key boundary lately?

Think about the week ahead.

How can you practice setting a boundary every day?

Monday

Tuesday

Wednesday

Thursday

Friday

Saturday

Sunday

What will you do with your one life?